# WE ARE THE MUSIC MAKERS!

## PRESERVING THE SOUL OF AMERICA'S MUSIC

### PICTURES & STORIES BY TIMOTHY & DENISE DUFFY

*"Through the efforts of the Music Maker Relief Foundation, these amazing people and artists have been able to live dignified lives. In many cases, they were rediscovered during their golden years by Tim and Denise Duffy, then given the joy of new recognition by their families, peers and fans world-over!* **- Taj Mahal**

# WE ARE THE MUSIC MAKERS!

## PRESERVING THE SOUL OF AMERICA'S MUSIC

### PICTURES & STORIES BY TIMOTHY & DENISE DUFFY

Copyright ©2014 Music Maker Relief Foundation. All rights reserved.

Published by The Nautilus Publishing Company

Nautilus Press
426 S. Lamar Blvd., Suite 16
Oxford, MS 38655
Tel: 662-513-0159
Fax: 662-234-9266
www.nautiluspublishing.com

ISBN 978-1-936946-28-0

Printed in China by Everbest Printing through an arrangement with
Four Colour Print Group, Louisville, Kentucky

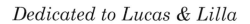

*Dedicated to Lucas & Lilla*

*"We are the music makers,*
*And we are the dreamers of dreams,*
*Wandering by lone sea-breakers,*
*And sitting by desolate streams;*
*World-losers and world-forsakers,*
*On whom the pale moon gleams:*
*Yet we are the movers and shakers*
*Of the world for ever, it seems."*

**- Arthur O'Shaughnessy, 1874**

## INTRODUCTION

DEBORAH & NEAL PATTMAN,
HASKELL "WHISTLIN'
   BRITCHES" THOMPSON,
MACAVINE HAYES,
LITTLE PINK ANDERSON,
COOTIE STARK,
CAPTAIN LUKE
   (LUTHER B. MAYER),
MR. Q (CUSELLE SETTLE),
WILLA MAE BUCKNER,
TIMOTHY DUFFY

CHARLOTTE, NC

America tells its stories through song. Consolation to the lovelorn, courage to the oppressed, warning to the naive or a ticket to the Promised Land, a great song can deliver the wisdom of ages directly to our souls.

Deeply personal and implausibly universal, the blues, jazz, gospel and old time music of the American South form a deep aquifer that contemporary musicians all around the world drink from daily. The music is constantly expanding and morphing into country, rock, rap and soul, but trace the origins and you will find yourself standing squarely in the South.

We romanticize the bluesman as the lone wolf and rambler, bringing his song into our dreary workaday world, but the taproot of American song has always survived on the sweat of working class brows. It is the offspring of the tenant farmer, factory worker and domestic servant born during the precious few leisure hours they shared with their communities at a Friday night fish fry, Saturday afternoon on the back porch, or on Sunday morning in their church clothes. In the days when openly expressing rage at injustice could cost a black man his life, gospel and blues developed a language known only to its initiates, a code that mocked the oppressors and fortified the common man with camaraderie and resolve to keep his eyes on the prize. While individual experiences with race, relationships, poverty, and work vary, the feelings of being subject to injustice or finding love at last are universal.

In the following pages, we present portraits of these artists: fathers and mothers, uncles and aunts, daughters and sons, grandparents and neighbors, who continue to lovingly stir the South's musical stew and feed American culture. You probably won't recognize their names or faces, for few have found fame. Most of them weren't easy to find.

My husband, Tim Duffy, has traveled the world with a guitar, tape recorder and camera since he was a college freshman in 1981. He started by documenting old time mountain musicians at weekly "pickin' parties" in western North Carolina. He finished his college degree studying the Swahili and their Tarabu music on the Kenyan coast. When he returned to America, he enrolled in a Masters program in the Curriculum of Folklore at the University of North Carolina, Chapel Hill. One of his last assignments was an oral history of James "Guitar Slim" Stephens, an African American blues artist from Greensboro, NC who was dying of cancer. Slim encouraged Tim to seek out Guitar Gabriel in Winston-Salem, NC. Tim began his search in the drink houses of East Winston where he discovered musical geniuses; he has continued to seek talent in dozens of housing projects, small towns, and farming communities from the Virginia Tidewater to East Texas.

To hear and record the most authentic, archaic musical forms, Tim always seeks out the oldest guy who learned from the oldest guy who came before. He has found that you can't just turn up on someone's doorstep one afternoon and expect them to bare their soul to your camera and recorder. Tim acknowledges a deep obligation to these artists, *"It is no small thing to ask a musician for their song and their story. The only way we can hope to make an equal exchange is if the documentarian and the artist have a genuine relationship; they must share more than just the moment the photo is taken or the song is captured."*

Tim took these photographs over the past twenty years and insists, *"I know who I am looking at through the lens."* He knows them because of the countless hours spent with each artist over months and years. Days spent sharing songs, food, laughter and far too many miles in vans and airplanes have built the bridges of trust that allow these artists to give their wisdom and art so generously. These artists share their life lessons with us because we are dedicated to presenting their music to the world with reverence and to be partners in their struggle for a better life.

Whether in Appalachia or Africa, the other constant companion to roots music is grinding, relentless poverty. On some visits the artist couldn't play for us because their guitar was in the pawnshop, or they weren't up to it because they had a splitting headache from not being able to buy blood pressure medication. Whenever we meet new artists, they never ask for a handout, but always, *"Do you know where I can get a gig? I need more work."*

We concluded that our nation's musical traditions were suffering from starvation and underemployment. We founded the Music Maker Relief Foundation as a nonprofit in 1994 to preserve America's music by directly supporting the people who make the music. We get gigs for those that want to perform, guitars for those who want to play, and feed the hungry. Our initial grassroots effort to meet the needs of a handful of blues musicians in Winston-Salem, NC, has grown to assist hundreds through the generosity and passion of our supporters, employees and volunteers.

We, in turn, have come to rely on the wisdom and knowledge of these elders in our personal and professional lives. We see the rebellions, loves, sorrows and joys these cultural treasures express in their stories, songs and pictures as reflections of our identity as the American people.

This book is filled with photographs of individuals we greatly respect and admire. Although an enthusiastic student of photography, Tim is a visual artist of necessity. He documents his surroundings because he is keenly aware that time is fleeting and these moments with elderly artists are too precious to be lost.

He focuses his lens entirely on Music Maker artists and our family. He does not guard these artists jealously, and often invites accomplished professionals to photograph these musicians. He asks the photographers to share their images with the artists, so they can be used to further their careers.

Tim shares his work with you here in hopes you will look more closely at the unrecognized greatness that surrounds you. He asks that you seek out the everyday heroic acts of art that will enrich your life.

**- Denise Duffy**

We would like to thank the artists of Music Maker Relief Foundation (Music Maker) for their love, kindness, and friendship, and for filling our lives with song.

Dear Rick, Kathleen, Nathaniel, JP, Dave and Betty, your faith and support are the cornerstones on which our foundation has been built. Please know we are grateful to all of you each day for the opportunity to do this work we love so well.

We are very grateful to the dedicated professionals who have volunteered their time and expertise to serve on our Board of Directors, including Mark Levinson, Lucy DeVries Duffy, Kay Hill, Spike Barkin, Glenn Hinson, Lightnin Wells, Mudcat, Bill Lucado, Bill Puckett, John Price, Taj Mahal, Henry Slyker, Ryan Costello, Blane Wright, Eric Ashman, Ann Pitts, Bart Farrell, Tom Meyer, Rhiannon Giddens, Dom Flemons, Justin Robinson, Rich Henneberry, Rick Teller, Catherine Elkins, Saramel Evans, Jon Porter, Tom Wallack and Mark Chatinsky.

## ACKNOWLEDGEMENTS

DENISE & TIM DUFFY,

SYLVESTER, GA

We would like to recognize our Advisory Board members for the support and wisdom they have generously shared, and give sincere thanks to Dickey Betts, Jackson Browne, Eric Clapton, Pura Fé Crescioni, Ardie Dean, Lutz Engelhart, Sue Foley, Ruthie Foster, Colonel Bruce Hampton, Jerry Harrison, Jimmy Herring, B.B King, Bill Krasilovsky, Mark Levinson, Tift Merritt, Jean-Hervé Michel, Bonnie Raitt, Tom Rankin, Kenny Wayne Shepherd, Ken Shepherd, Susan Tedeschi, Dr. David Thurber, Pete Townshend, Derek Trucks, and Don Was.

Bringing musicians and music lovers together to experience and celebrate live performance is the most rewarding part of our work. We thank the many festivals, venues and corporate sponsors that have made these experiences possible including Cathead Vodka, Clyde's Restaurant Group, RJ Reynolds, Volkswagen of America, Legendary Rhythm and Blues Cruise, Lugano Blues to Bop, Roots N' Blues N' BBQ Festival, New Orleans Jazz & Heritage Festival, Byron Bay Blues Festival, Lincoln Center Out of Doors Series, NC Museum of History, Mississippi Valley Blues Festival, The Hamilton and The Crescent City Blues Festival.

We offer our deepest appreciation to the thousands of music lovers who have joined us on this journey and supported Music Maker with their contributions. We are humbled and grateful for the support given by the National Endowment for the Arts, NC Arts Council, NC Humanities Council, Mid-Atlantic Arts Council, Strowd Roses Foundation, Blues Music Foundation, Orange Arts Commission, Mary Duke Biddle Foundation, George Shields Foundation, and the many generous family foundations that have contributed to the growth of this mission over the past twenty years.

Many people have joined us on this journey including family members who have embraced this mission from the outset: Tim's dear mother Lucy Devries, Dan, Sam and Paul Duffy and Diane and Lou Durocher. John Evans of Jackson, MS. Axel Küstner who dedicated his life to documenting American blues musicians and inspired Tim to take photography seriously. We acknowledge the southern folklife fieldworkers Paul Clayton, Alan Lomax, George Mitchell, Bill Ferris, Bruce Bastin, Peter B. Lowery, Glenn Hinson, David Evans, and Kip Lornell, whose work led us to many great artists. Photographer Mark Austin has been our dedicated artistic and technical advisor. Musical director Ardie Dean has dedicated his career to supporting our artists in performing and recording since 1991! Our thanks go to Katharine Walton for telling us to write this book together.

We thank Ken Toda of Huemax for supplying cameras, equipment and instruction on all aspects of photography and to Bill Moretz of Pro Camera for his expert advice on many aspects of photography.

Simon Archache, our Photo Editor, scanned 1200 negatives and reviewed thousands of digital images for our final review. Raphael Everard put together all the sound recordings of our 20th Anniversary compilation CD, which is a companion to this book. Christine Shia transcribed Tim's recorded reflections. Our interns, Thomas Ciaburri, Swathi Mohan, Thomas Heisler, Emily Urquhart and Margot Pien all spent months helping us develop this book. We thank Polly Beere for her invaluable help editing, Dom Flemons for his advice, Bruno Boussard for designing this book and Elena Rott for retouching the photographs.

We depend on the passion, dedication and talents of Music Maker's staff daily to keep our organization moving forward. Communications and Development Coordinator Corinne Everett Belch's dedication and organizational skills keep us all on track. Aaron Greenhood, Artist Services Coordinator, has led the effort to organize our photographic archives and partnered in creating the Tintype images of Major Handy, Cary Morin, Pat Wilder and Dom Flemons. Margot Pien researched the biographical information on the artists. Cornelius Lewis dons whichever hat we need him to and Janet Askew keeps the bills paid so we can keep creating.

We are grateful to the University of North Carolina, Chapel Hill, and Steve Weiss for creating the Timothy Duffy Collection at the Southern Folklife Collection at Wilson Library, where the master tapes and photographic collection are archived in perpetuity.

Cora Mae Bryant, Cootie Stark, Captain Luke, Willa Mae Buckner, Macavine Hayes

Pinnacle, NC

*"Blues is a legend, it is something that will be with us out through the generations. It explains your up-haps and misfortunes, good-haps, the people you have been around, the people you associate with and the things that happened to you in your life.*
*You can go to university, school, college, but if you do not learn it in the street, walking through life, you will never really learn it. That is what blues is all about, it is a feeling, you don't find it on notes and paper, it comes from the heart."* **- Guitar Gabriel**

## Tim Duffy & Guitar Gabriel

Utrecht, Holland 1991

In 1991, when I was 28 years old, I dedicated myself to locating "undiscovered" blues artists that lived in and around Winston-Salem, NC. When I knocked on Guitar Gabriel's door, he hobbled out, hugged me and said, "Boy, I know where you want to go. I have been there before. I will take you there but my time ain't long. I want you to promise me that when I die, you'll bury me with my guitar."

I began to book gigs and to record his music. At the same time I brought Gabe to the doctor and he introduced me to his musician friends. Every month on check day, I drove him and these elder musicians around town to pay their bills. I saw firsthand how their money always ran out before the last bill was paid or the groceries were bought.

Poverty's continual assault on these musicians' ability to create and share their art inspired the creation of the Music Maker Relief Foundation.

## Captain Luke (Luther B. Mayer)

HILLSBOROUGH, NC 1994

Captain Luke has a voice like honey dripping on hot chocolate. He was Guitar Gabriel's best friend and companion. For decades, they were the kings of the Drink House circuit in Winston-Salem, NC.

Their favorite hang was Ezelle's, which was open 24 hours a day, 7 days a week, and it's where I met many musicians, including Captain Luke, Willa Mae Buckner, Mr. Q and Macavine Hayes. Ezelle ran this place for 40 years and since he would grant credit to working folks, his joint was a center of community life.

When I first knocked on the Drink House doors they would be shut in my face; being young and white, folks assumed that I must be the police. When I met Captain Luke in 1991 he took me around for a year until I was welcomed with big smiles at all the local establishments.

## Macavine Hayes

Pinnacle, NC 2006

Part court jester, part gut-bucket blues master, Macavine Hayes was nobody's fool. The witty wisdom imparted through his gravely spoken parables and poetry confounded many and kept the rest of us in stitches. Always the last one to go to bed and the first one up in the morning, Mac's zest for life on the road and his hauntingly primitive guitar style were the personification of blues in its rawest form.

## Willa Mae Buckner and Siam

WINSTON-SALEM, NC 1994

At age 14, in 1936, Willa Mae Buckner ran away from her home in Decatur, GA, and joined an all black carnival. Over the years, she painted her body gold and posed, was a contortionist, laid on a bed of nails, danced in the chorus line, sang with the band, and later was a burlesque dancer at the Midnight Rambles. In the early 1960s she launched her traveling snake show with 26 snakes and a chimpanzee. She drove her show around in a panel truck with the snakes in cages in the back and her chimp up front, riding shotgun. She would often stop on a country road and let all the snakes out for a walk. When she wanted to get them back in the truck, she would hide behind a bush. The snakes would look for "Mama" and not seeing her would quickly slither back into their cages. When I met her in 1991 she lived with two 18-foot pythons that roamed her house freely. Willa communicated with them by tapping her foot: they would come to her when she "called" and she would feed them frozen rats directly from her hand.

*One day when I visited her, she called me into her bedroom to see something special.*
*She lifted up her bed pillow and there were ten baby pythons coiled around her Smith & Wesson.*
*She cackled, "Do you think anyone is going to mess with me?" Willa was one of our first artists*
*and we made her lifelong dream come true when she performed her hilarious risqué songs*
*in a Circus Blues show at Carnegie Hall in 1993.*

**Mr. Q** (Cuselle Settle)

Pinnacle, NC 1994

Mr. Q's father wore a suit and tie when he plowed the fields walking behind his mule. While Mr. Q followed his Daddy's lead and was always impeccably dressed, as a teenager he ran away from his home in Winston-Salem, NC to join Blanche Calloway's big band.

In the 1940s, he landed in New York City and immersed himself in the jazz scene of the post Harlem Renaissance. He played harmonica with the Savoy Sultans, was a prize winning Lindy Hop dancer and became a professional entertainer singing and playing the piano.

*He bought this hat during the 1970s, and every spring he would give it a fresh coat of paint. Red one year, green the next; by the time I met up with him, it weighed more than an Army helmet.*

## Samuel Turner Stevens & Tim Duffy

Leicester, NC 1998

When I first moved to Asheville as a college student in 1981, I went to visit Sam because of his great reputation among area musicians. I pulled up in his driveway but the grass had not been cut in years and I stood there not knowing where to go. Sam stuck his head out of a concrete block shop so I offered a hello. He replied, "You sound like a Yankee," and stepped back inside. I persisted and despite my Northern heritage we became fast friends.

I began spending most of my weekends and school nights over at Sam's drinking beer, playing guitar and sleeping on an old van bench in his kitchen. Sam was an "authentic DIY guy." He made his own fiddles, he made his own banjos, he made his own windmill, and he made his own moonshine.

As a kid, Sam traveled deep into the mountain hollers of Western North Carolina and Eastern Tennessee with the legendary song-catcher Bascom Lamar Lunsford. As a result Sam had an enormous repertoire of folk songs and archaic fiddle and banjo techniques that are hard to come by anymore.

*"A preacher came to dinner and told my mother*
*he wanted to give her a 'holy kiss'!"*

**Big Boy Henry**
Beaufort, NC 1994

I first saw Big Boy Henry at a small club in Chapel Hill, NC. In the middle of a song, he jerked up his head to let out a moan and his dentures shot out of his mouth and slid clear across the floor towards the audience. He did not miss a beat and kept singing. I handed him his teeth; he slid them in his shirt pocket, shook my hand and asked me if I played. I told him I did and he nodded at me to pick up his guitar and then broke into song. Big Boy treated everybody like they were somebody.

Big Boy was a vivid storyteller with a wry wit that told it like it was with lines such as: "Oh Bellevina, you done got old and you done got ugly, but I love you anyway."

## Etta Baker

Etta Baker was the modern master of Piedmont Blues. Her versions of "One-Dime Blues" and "Railroad Bill" became standards during the Folk Revival in the 1960s after folk-singer Paul Clayton produced the hugely successful "Instrumental Music of the Southern Appalachians." This record has been in print since 1959. Etta was invited to the Newport Folk Festival but her husband would not let her go. Etta was a beautiful woman, and he wasn't taking any chances. After he passed away in 1976 she quit her decades-long job in the cotton mill and began her performing career.

When we began working with her, Etta was already 80 years old. We were able to get her the first, only and thankfully large royalty payment for her early recordings. We helped reinvigorate a very active and successful career in the 1990s. Her first album with Music Maker, "Railroad Bill," stands as a classic. She recorded two more albums for us and appeared in several documentaries. She returned to the banjo at the age of 89 because it reminded her of the father she adored. She finished recording her last record at the age of 91, and passed away soon after.

## John Dee Holeman

DURHAM, NC 2011

*"I caught it from my cousin, who caught it from my uncle,*
*who caught it from Blind Boy Fuller."*
John Dee reflected on how he was infected with the blues.

Raised on a tobacco farm in Orange County, NC, John Dee exemplifies the Southern blues gentleman. Always impeccably dressed and dignified, John will sit in front of his audience and play the most down home country blues you will ever hear. He was very proud when he shared a bill in Durham with his idol Lightnin' Hopkins. Lightnin' sat right in front as John Dee played, just smiling. Afterwards he told John Dee that it was the best blues he had heard in many years.

## Algia Mae Hinton

North Carolina farm girl Algia Mae Hinton raised seven children on her own after her husband died at a young age. Widowhood did not slow down her step and she earned a North Carolina Folk Heritage Award for her buck dancing and for writing songs such as, "Cook Cornbread for your Husband and Biscuits for your Outside Man" and "If You Kill a Chicken, Save Me the Head!"

When she got happy, she would play the guitar behind her head and begin to buck dance. She recorded one of the most lonesome blues songs ever by humming into a comb with a piece of paper laid on top, while her good friends Taj Mahal and Etta Baker finger picked their guitars.

**George Higgs**

George was a Piedmont bluesman. He grew up farming in a little Carolina hamlet called Speed – "a fast name for a slow town," he used to joke.

When he was young, he traded a hound dog for his neighbor's guitar. The hound dog came back home, but George kept the guitar.

# J.C. McCool

Black Mountain, NC 2004

J.C. McCool composed the fiddle standard "The Black Mountain Rag." He began his career when he was just ten years old playing with Walter Davis and Clarence Greene; they recorded in the 1930s as The Blue Ridge Mountain Entertainers.

When I first came to Swannanoa, NC in 1981 to go to college, I was introduced to Walt Davis, Ray Greene and J.C. by my new fiddler friend Jeff Robbins. We went out to Ray's on the weekends and helped him build a cinderblock building in his backyard. There, Ray hosted a pickin' party for old time musicians to get together and play every Monday night ever since, for more than 20 years.

After I started Music Maker, I visited J.C. and found him crippled with arthritis and nearly blind. He told us his fixed income was too little to afford groceries. We offered him a monthly stipend to help out. While he accepted the checks, he admitted being uncomfortable accepting money from an organization that primarily supported African American musicians. Several years later on another visit, he spoke his heart -- that after a lifetime of being prejudiced he had an awakening and changed churches to one that embraces all people. J.C. thanked us for being part of his enlightenment.

## Drink Small

COLUMBIA, SC 1995

*"A lot of guys who never been discovered will have a second chance now with your organization. Some of them that have been discovered but were about to give up, you spice them up, you give them something to live for, a reason to continue on. And for those that have done it and stopped, you give them something to come back to."*

Known as the "Blues Doctor," Drink Small plays a vast repertoire of blues: Delta, Piedmont, Chicago, Slide – the list goes on and on. Growing up in a family of musicians, he began playing the pump organ at eleven years old and learned the guitar from an old bluesman known only as Greenback.

## Haskell "Whistlin' Britches" Thompson

Winston-Salem, NC 1995

Whistlin' Britches' infectious joy and enthusiasm were all he had.

When he was young, he worked for a funeral home in Winston-Salem, NC. His job was to listen to the police scanner and the minute he heard there was an accident, to alert his crew and rush off to the scene.

Haskell would ride on the front bumper of the hearse, and upon arrival, would leap off and run to tag the body. Whichever mortuary's workers tagged the body first, it was the one that got the job of taking the body to the morgue or hospital.

Whistlin' Britches began "clicking" as a kid. The ring of the horseshoe hitting the metal made a "cling" and he tried to imitate that sound with his mouth. It became his signature percussion sound and his click was as loud as a rim shot on a snare drum.

*"I was born in the wrong part of the world and then again
I didn't go anyplace better. When you got a bad break like I had,
you doubt yourself. You know it's rough, man."*

**JW Warren**

Ariton, AL 1994

JW was his first name, not an abbreviation. In 1995, when I first knocked on his door, I had to talk to him through it for 45 minutes before he finally cracked it open and told me to come back the next day. Denise and I returned, we recorded his songs and became lasting friends. Music Maker sent him a beautiful guitar and helped him buy his medicine every month.

*"Zeigler's music is the last footprint of the African music before it took the next step into Southern music. His song 'Going Away' is a very deep and ancient piece of music."*

**- Taj Mahal**

## John Lee Zeigler & Denise Duffy

KATHLEEN, GA 1994

From Kathleen, GA, John Lee was raised on a farm with 17 siblings. He played the guitar left-handed, with the strings upside down, striking the bass strings with his index finger and the treble strings with his thumb.

Following George Mitchell's trail from 20 years earlier we pulled into Kathleen and stopped at the crossroads to inquire about John Lee at the gas station. John and his young wife were raising his four grandchildren in his very humble self-built home. He agreed to record a certain number of songs but to our dismay, he believed in only one take, even if the phone was ringing.

*"You got to have rain in your life to appreciate the sunshine."*

**Essie Mae Brooks**

Pinnacle, NC 2006

Essie Mae is an old time gospel songwriter from Perry, GA. As a young girl, she had visions of gospel songs while riding in a wagon with her father to Drumbeat gatherings. Essie Mae is known for her unique outlook on hardship.

Essie Mae brought two huge suitcases on tour to France. One of them took two of us to lift. A few days into this burden I asked her what was in the heavy suitcase. She replied, "I thought there might not be any good food here, so I packed up some canned goods. But you know, the food has been wonderful so far!" We opened it up to find dozens and dozens of cans of beanie weenies, potted meat, and Spaghetti-Os. Essie shared them with all the musicians, who were happy to have a taste of home.

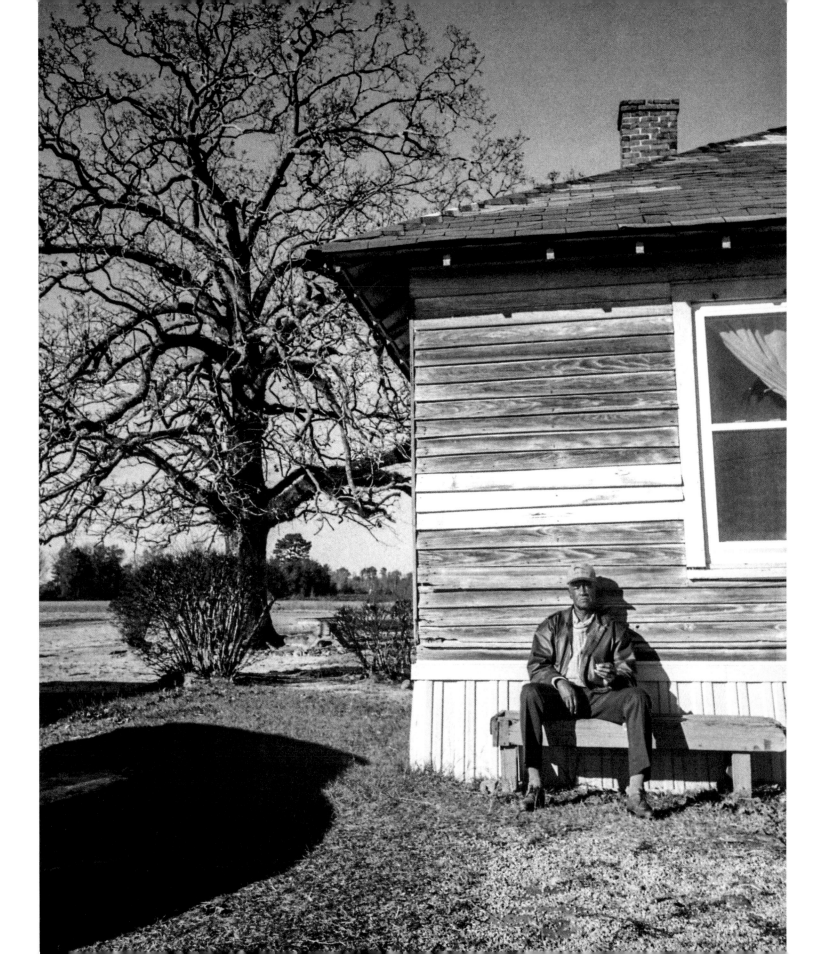

## Rufus McKenzie

Perry, GA 1996

Rufus McKenzie, from Perry, GA, sang in the ancient field holler tradition. He is one of the most amazing musicians I ever recorded.

**Slavery Time Blues**

*Well you know, my grandmother and my grandfather.*
*People, they're dead and in their graves.*
*They told me son, your grandparents both was slaves.*

*Well you know, they keep telling me that this country is free.*
*There's gonna be some changes in the White House 'cause people I don't see no freedom for me.*

*You know, I walked to my boss's house.*
*Knocked up on his back door. He said, "What can I do for you?"*
*I said please, please, boss man, give me a bite to eat.*

*You know, my boss man's wife she would fix me a plate. When I began to eat, she began to smile.*
*Big dog standing in the corner, people, he began to growl.*

*I said Lady, I am sorry, I am sorry I believe your dog has seen a snake.*
*She said no, no my friend, you are eating from his plate.*

*And you still want to know, why the black man sings the blues?*
*You know, there has been so many a cold morning, people, I had to go to work without no shoes.*

## James Davis

PERRY, GA 1995

"Drumbeat" is a style of music that enslaved Africans developed in middle Georgia; after emancipation, the Davis family remained in the area. The men in James Davis's family have been playing this music for generations. His father played the bass drum, his uncle the snare drum accompanied by the fife. James played electric guitar accompanied by a trap set drummer. DRUMBEAT was the only word on his handbills, everyone knew where to show up every Saturday night and dance.

**W.C Minger III**

PINNACLE, NC 1995

Bill was a poet, guitarist and fruit tramp from the great Northwest. When I was 16, I met Bill and a number of young working class songwriters in an apple orchard in Dryden, WA. Their songs were as important to me as any of the classic folk recordings on my dad's shelf back home.

**Home on the Range**

*She wanted a home where the buffalo roam*
*Where the deer and the antelope play*
*But I too often heard those discouraging words*
*You're a drifter! You're a rounder! You're a stray!*
*In spite of your wishes, I'll never do dishes*
*And I often stay cloudy all day*
*My ranch is a backpack and*
*My range is a train track*
*So to hell with your home on the range*

*"We need the Music Maker, not the Undertaker!"*

**Jerry "Boogie" McCain**

GADSDEN, AL 1995

Denise and I met "Boogie" in 1995 and we made an acoustic record in a nearby hotel room. When we finished the session, I asked Jerry, "After so many decades of bad record deals, what would make you happy?" He replied, "I want a $10,000 advance and I will make a GREAT electric blues record."

I shelved our humble recording and in 1999, I arranged a deal with Cello Recordings. Jerry got his advance, was backed up by Stevie Ray Vaughn's drummer and bassist, "Double Trouble," and he created the greatest album of his career, "This Stuff Just Kills Me."

**Precious Bryant** & Lucas Duffy

<small>WARM SPRINGS, GA 1998</small>

*"Precious had a way of immediately
pulling you into her soul! I'll never forget
the first time I heard her, I knew I could never
get enough of how she sang, her voice and the
intimate wisdom with which she chose topics for
her songs! Just so achingly perfect and all at
once beautiful and personal!"*

**- Taj Mahal**

## Taj Mahal

Durham, NC 1998

Taj Mahal has been the greatest torchbearer of blues and world music for the last 50 years. His early partnership with guitarist Jesse Ed Davis showed the way and earned the respect of iconic groups such as The Allman Brothers, The Rolling Stones, John Lennon and so many more. His pioneering work in revealing the connections between the musical traditions from the Americas, Africa, the Caribbean and the South Pacific has now become known as World Music.

Growing up learning the blues of Mississippi and North Carolina from neighborhood friends in Springfield, MA, the blues remain at the root of this maestro's compositions. When he heard of Music Maker, he immediately joined the mission, visited the artists, recorded and took them on tour around the country. Without his devotion, advice and mentorship, we would not have been able to grow and sustain so many artists.

## George & Lula Daniels

SOCIETY HILL, AL 2011

Denise and I were on the road to Society Hill, AL, to visit Robert Thomas's place in the backwoods where there was no electricity, no telephone, and no running water. The smoke hung thick over the scattered patches of black-water swamp. As we pulled into his shack there was no one home except a one-eyed Bluetick hound. We headed down to George Daniels' place a few miles away. George is a bluesman and he may have the rankest electric guitar sound in the South. His amp is a living hell, but he is a great singer and harmonica player when we could get him to unplug his guitar. He offered us some of his homemade rye whiskey before he started into his ear-splittingly loud blues.

George was a cowboy in northern Alabama working cattle for the same boss till their family died out. After this visit in 1996 we began helping him with a monthly sustenance grant. This photo was taken on a visit in 2011, when we discovered he had gone blind. He told us he was sitting around waiting for his sight to come back: he seemed completely certain that it would. He is still waiting.

## Cora Fluker

Cora Fluker was born in Livingston, AL, around 1920 into a family of sharecroppers. The conditions on the plantation were so hard that she tried to run away at the age of nine, only to be caught and dragged back by the white landowner and beaten nearly to death. She showed us the scars on her back and was deeply haunted by this awful memory. In her teens she was struggling with her faith, and in prayer, she had a vision of Jesus and henceforth devoted her life to preaching. In the 1940s her family moved to Marion, MS, and she began her ministry. She built her own church on the family land. She would travel from town to town singing her original gospel songs and preaching on street corners. Cora had the most powerful voice we have ever recorded.

# Carl Hodges

SALUDA, VA 2005

Carl Hodges was part of the rare Chesapeake Bay blues tradition. He grew up sharecropping in Saluda, VA and loved to dig holes as a young boy. Once he dug a hole so deep that he could not get out and had to spend the night down in the ground before his parents found him. He spent his career hand-digging wells.

*"Blues is a deep testimony, the blues is something that you can express yourself.*
*People don't realize the meaning of the blues. The blues is something that came from way back.*
*The younger generation and the older generation please don't forget where you come from!*
*The blues, the old shackles have built the road to travel on y'all. Please don't throw the blues away.*
*Because my grandfather, my grandmother have struggled the hard way to bring you all forth here.*
*They had to get up early in the morning, sometimes the moon would be shining as bright as day,*
*sometimes it would be so dark and they would have to go out to the well and draw water,*
*let the old bucket down. The blues has studied the old rope and the chain.*
*We didn't have what we have today."*

## Cootie Stark

GREENVILLE, SC 1997

When I met Cootie he had been playing on street corners since he was a teenager. Totally blind since his late 20s, he had never let go of his dream of making it with his music. He performed very old blues that he had learned from his uncle and musicians with the names of Blind Simmie Dooley, Chilly Wind, Reverend Gary Davis, Peg Leg Sam, Pink Anderson, Walter Phelps and Josh White in Cootie's home of Greenville, SC.

Launching a new career initiative at the age of 71 with Music Maker, Cootie toured and recorded with Taj Mahal, played throughout Europe and became an overnight success after 50 years of hard work.

## Neal Pattman

Athens, GA 1995

Neal loved his blues and would sing and play his harp anywhere. I always got a kick when he broke into a gospel song every time we were about to take off on a plane. On a trip with Cootie, the three of us had to catch a train in Paris. Cootie just walked up to get up on the train, but — being completely blind — did not step far enough and disappeared off of the platform edge into the gap. Neal jumped up, landed in a knee squat and reached down deep with his one arm and pulled him up so hard that Cootie popped up like a cork and landed on his feet, just inside the train's door!

## Benton Flippen

MOUNT AIRY, NC 2006

A prominent musician on Mount Airy's WPAQ since the 1940s, Benton's fiddle tunes are played by musicians worldwide. He played for square dances every weekend in Surry County, NC until his passing at the age of 91. When we were located in Pinnacle, Benton lived just a few miles away. He would come to our summer picnics and just loved playing his bluesy fiddle with all the other Music Maker artists. He would be the first to start playing and the last one to stop.

## Beverly "Guitar" Watkins

ATLANTA, GA 1995

In 1995 I met Beverly "Guitar" Watkins performing in the Atlanta Undergound for tips. I was blown away to see a Southern grandma play a fierce electric guitar. No reason that she shouldn't. She began with the original Dr. Feelgood in 1959, cutting records that John Lennon said influenced his work. Beverly joined Music Maker and toured the US with Taj Mahal in 1998 and 1999. In the years that followed, she also toured with our ensemble in Argentina, Australia and throughout Europe.

**Cora Mae Bryant**

The daughter of Georgia guitar legend Curley Weaver told us about her childhood: "When I grew up sharecropping, there was no difference between white and black. We were all poor together out there in the fields. We had oil lamp lights, the only food we got from the store was coffee and sugar. When daddy came around I would follow him from house party to house party, meeting up with his friends Blind Willie McTell and Buddy Moss, we would go out three, sometimes four days at a time without sleeping a wink."

Cora was a great blues singer and prolific songwriter.

*"If it ain't been in the pawn shop, it can't play the blues."*

**- Frank Edwards**

**Mr. Frank Edwards**  & Cool John Ferguson

HILLSBOROUGH, NC 2002

Mr. Frank Edwards bought his first guitar at age 12. His father was a "Terrible Christian" and forbade him to play and smashed his instrument. Frank left home that day; he was 14 years old, moved to St. Augustine, FL, and never saw his old man again. Frank hoboed across the country performing. He recorded for Okeh Records in 1940, Regal Records in 1949, Trix Records in 1973, and Music Maker in 2004.

This photo was taken after he recorded his last song; three hours later he died at 93 years of age of a heart attack near Greenville, SC en route to his home in Atlanta, GA.

## Carl Rutherford

PINNACLE, NC 1998

Carl grew up coal mining in War, WV. He migrated to California as a young man to work in the lumber mills, making a home with his new wife and another fellow in a hollowed out Redwood stump. Many years later, he moved back to the old home place and wrote incredible songs.

**Turn Off The Fear**

*You got to turn off the fear when you come down into here*
*When you're down here loading coal for the man*
*You cannot be worried about things that can go wrong*
*You got to keep loading coal and plodding along*
*A man's life ain't worth nothing, at least that's how it seems*
*There is just muscle and guts under these machines*
*When the rock starts to falling, the boss man says "Son,*
*You better bring out my machine, don't ya leave it and run*
*You got kin and your loved ones that are waiting back home*
*They're depending upon you for everything y'all own."*
*So with the mud and dripping top and that old dust in the air*
*You got to turn off the fear when you come into here*
*When you're working in the dark coal mine*
*You got to know that your dear Lord is holding you near*
*And turn off the fear when you come down into here.*

## Cool John Ferguson

After Guitar Gabriel died, Captain Luke called me up and told me we needed another guitar player. He remembered a talented guy that he used to see traveling with a Gospel group and he thought the fellow lived in Beaufort, SC.

I found Cool John Ferguson by calling up the historic Penn Center on the island of St. Helena and that is where we met a few weeks later. Cool John can play in any style; if he does not know it he will figure it out within minutes. There is nothing rote about his music; he drinks deep from the ever-flowing black river of music. He moved up to North Carolina and lived near the Music Maker studio for six years, backing up artists on dozens of recordings artists with true inspiration.

The lore is that Cool John was born knowing how to play the guitar: he just had to wait for his hands to grow big enough to get around the neck. He was leading his church band at the age of five.

*"I've never tried to build churches, I try to build my faith."*

## Elder Anderson Johnson

Religion and music were a part of Elder Anderson Johnson's life for as long as he could remember; he began playing the guitar at six years old. He experienced the first taste of success when he was living in Miami, FL, singing with his steel guitar on a vacant lot on Second Street. A man from a local record company recorded Elder Johnson as he laid down his popular rendition of "God Don't Like It." The song went on to be released on the Angel, Glory and Deluxe labels. He eventually settled down in his hometown of Newport News, VA, founded his own church and built a faithful congregation. He also concentrated on his visual art, gaining recognition as an outsider artist.

Axel Küstner introduced me to Elder Anderson. He was forever thankful; although he was a world renowned visual artist, no one had ever paid much attention to his music. Axel and I were amazed when we recorded him in 1994 that his voice and guitar playing were as strong as they had been in recordings from the 1950s.

## Willie King

ALICEVILLE, AL 2003

Born in rural Mississippi, Willie moved to Chicago to pursue his blues but later returned home to Pickens County, AL, deep in the country. He was dedicated to social change and to the children in his impoverished homeland. He led his nonprofit, the Rural Members Association, teaching music, quilting and gardening to "at risk" kids in the summer. We donated instruments of all kinds to this program and helped his Freedom Creek Festival by sponsoring the performances of the elder blues musicians in the community.

# Birmingham George Conner

ALICEVILLE, AL 1997

Late one night, I drove down miles and miles of dirt road, beyond the electrical grid in rural Pickens County, AL to reach Birmingham George's juke joint. George ran jukes in Chicago and Memphis as a young man before returning to his native Alabama. A generator hummed in the darkness; it powered a loud stereo blaring down-home blues. The front yard of hard clay hosted dozens of men and women doing a dance they called the Watusi. He called his moonshine "Jack Dempsey," as it had a knock-out punch.

**Othar Turner** & Shardé Thomas

ALICEVILLE, AL 1996

Othar Turner of Gravel Springs, MS led the Rising Star Fife and Drums Corps for decades.

Here at Willie King's Freedom Creek Festival he was 90 years old and his young granddaughter Shardé was blowing the fife like a prodigy

## Jack Owens

Jack Owens of Bentonia, MS played his blues in an eerie minor key. On his first trip overseas to perform in Holland, he got stopped going through security because Jack always kept a pistol in his boot. Security made Jack's friend David Evans put the gun back in the car before allowing them to get on the plane.

## Eddie Tigner

ATLANTA, GA 2005

Eddie Tigner enlisted in the Army and was stationed in Baltimore with two of the greatest guitar players of all time, Les Paul and T-Bone Walker. After the Army, Eddie returned to his native Atlanta and spent a year backing up blues icon Elmore James. From the 1950s through the 1980s nearly every Holiday Inn in America had a music lounge featuring live music. An elegant musician and consummate professional, Eddie played most of them. For 35 years he led an Ink Spots group on tour throughout our nation.

He told me, "I played every Army Base in the US and countless ones overseas. At one time, we had five groups traveling the country as The Ink Spots."

We met Eddie in 1996 when he had retired from the road and was working in a school cafeteria. We helped him record a new album, and at the age of 86 he still performs often and travels on occasion.

## George Herbert Moore

Pinnacle, NC 1998

George grew up in Burgaw, a town just north of Wilmington, NC. He worked much of his life as a farmer and sawmill operator but always played his blues. In 1992, in his 70s, he began performing his first shows beyond his community. When we granted him this beautiful Gibson *Les Paul* guitar, he told us it was his proudest moment.

*"God woke me up this morning and started me on my way.*
*He didn't have to do it, but he done it."*

**- Elder James Goins**

**Mother Pauline & Elder James Goins**

Driving from a show in Charleston, SC, Denise and I took the back roads home. We stopped in Ridgeway, SC at an interesting curio shop. I asked the owner if he knew any old musicians. He made a call, and the next thing we knew, up rolled Elder James and Mother Pauline Goins. We set up our gear and recorded their very old sound, which was rooted in a combination of ancient African string music and the earliest African American gospel.

## Albert Smith

Albert Smith was a soft-spoken man, powerful gospel shouter and church pianist. He began playing the piano in 1927, when his parents bought him one from the Sears and Roebuck catalog. He was an inspiration to musicians such as Drink Small, who was his neighbor. Albert lived on his family's old farm and made a living giving piano lessons and making music in church. When we met him his piano was in terrible shape. The next week we sent a good used piano and he just loved it. We visited him many times and recorded hours of gospel and blues songs. He was offered shows throughout the country, but he refused every one, "I'm not much for traveling, I like being around home."

**Clyde Langford** & **High Steppin' Momma**

In 1999, a supporter sent me an article about the bluesman Clyde Langford from Midway, TX, a town between Dallas and Houston. I called him up, and discovered a really nice man with a lilting Texas accent. I told him that he reminded me of Lightnin' Hopkins and Clyde said Lightnin's family used to live right across the road from him.

We granted Clyde this beautiful Stratocaster guitar. Soon after, I visited him at his home and recorded 50 songs; they are some of the most unusual arrangements of old blues standards you will ever hear.

## Joe Lee Cole

Delta Blues is filled with lore about its beginnings in toil and misery. For many artists the hardships have not been overcome. Joe lived outside of Clarksdale, MS in a tiny town called Bobo. His home was an old shack with one light bulb. To me, Joe Lee represents the thousands of unknown Southern artists whose work is only known to their families and communities, and I was lucky to get a glimpse of this man.

## Macavine Hayes & Little Freddie King

Porto, Portugal 2006

One of the most significant things we can offer Music Maker partner artists is membership in our community of musicians. When these artists spend time together performing on the road, they are inspired to play their best, to pull out old material and to write new songs. The competition is genial and artists often form friendships and stay in touch between tours. This camaraderie often means as much to our senior artists as the financial support Music Maker provides.

## Adolphus Bell

Denise and I were coming back from Louisville, KY when we saw this van driving alongside of us and on it was painted "Adolphus Bell, One-Man Band." For three years I asked everyone I knew if they had heard of Adolphus Bell. Then our friend Mudcat called and told us he had just done a show with Adolphus in Birmingham, AL. We invited Adolphus to perform at the King Biscuit Blues Festival in Helena, AR. We sent him money to repair his van to make the trip. His show was magnificent and he began a deep partnership with Music Maker.

Adolphus named his guitar "Pawnshop" because it had been in pawn so many times. He insisted that each time he got it out, it sounded "even more bluesier."

When we met him, Adolphus had been homeless and living in his van for 15 years. Music Maker helped him build his career and soon he had an apartment, dentures, a new van, a recording and was touring Argentina, Australia, Europe and throughout the States. It took a few years but by 2009 his career was soaring; sadly he fell ill with lung cancer. Adolphus fought this disease valiantly and Music Maker remained by his side helping with medical and household needs during his four-year-long illness. His last wish was for "Pawnshop" to be sent up to Music Maker when he was gone, so it would keep playing the blues.

## Carolina Chocolate Drops,
**with Paul Martin, Connie Smith, Marty Stuart**

Nashville, TN 2009

The Grammy-winning Carolina Chocolate Drops (Rhiannon Giddens, Dom Flemons, Justin Robinson) learned their core repertoire from then 85-year old African American fiddler Joe Thompson of Mebane, NC. They revived the almost-forgotten black string band tradition and have performed this music to millions of music fans throughout the world. The founding members of the band serve on Music Makers Board of Directors.

*Country music legend Marty Stuart invited them to be the first black string band to ever perform on the Grand Ole Opry! When they received a standing ovation, Marty leaned over and told me, "That was a healing moment."*

**Pura Fé Crescioni**, Charly Lowry (left) & Ejo

HILLSBOROUGH, NC 2011

Our first meetings with Pura Fé forever changed our understanding of
Southern music history. Previously we had seen that history as a black and
white story. Pura Fé explained the intertwined lives and musical traditions
of African and Native Peoples in America.

*"We were bred together on slave plantations during colonization of our land.
Marooned colonies and the Underground Railroad ran through most of Indian-occupied
territory on old trade paths. This union gave birth to a rich new culture blending religion,
dance, food, good-looking people and the Blues. Charley Patton, the first King of the Blues
from Mississippi: he's Choctaw. Howlin Wolf heard and learned from Charley and recorded
tunes that Elvis Presley learned and recorded, who went on to change the world! Scrapper
Blackwell is Cherokee. Jimi Hendrix, Don Cherry, Duke Ellington, Thelonious Monk,
Lena Horne, Little Richard, Tina Turner, Chaka Khan, Jesse Ed Davis are just
a small list of musicians with a blended heritage who turned the course of popular
music in the last 100 years."*

**- Pura Fé Crescioni**

*"Your deeds, your deeds will bring you down."*

**David Butler**

Hillsborough, NC 2006

David spoke in deep Southern dialect and when he sang it took me awhile to figure out what he was singing about. When I did I realized he was a great poet. All his songs were messages on morality and how to live one's life. It seemed like he stepped out of the past with his colorful history of playing short stop in the Negro Leagues with the White Sox, making a living boxing in back lots, working as a brakeman on the railroad, riding his motorcycle across the country with his guitar, and growing up learning the blues from his father, who played piano with Tampa Red.

## Henry Byrd

SANFORD, FL 2003

I met Henry Byrd in Sanford, FL, when he was in his
80s. He was a retired construction worker who still played
true Piedmont Blues. Blind Boy Fuller, the founding father
of Piedmont Blues, taught him how to play. They would meet
on the streets of Durham, NC, where Henry often visited.

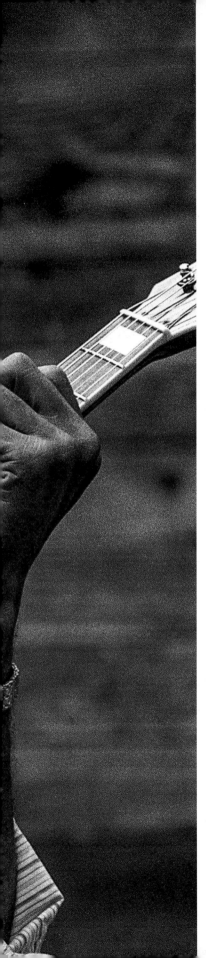

"What Can an Old Man Do But Sing the Blues" seemed a fitting title track for the debut album Dr. Burt cut at the age of 72. His music conveys the ample heartache, hope, progress and hardships he faced during the struggle for civil rights. As a citizen of Birmingham, AL, Dr. Burt lived through the segregated bussing and church bombings and managed to escape death when he was shot while leading a march. Soon after, he did hard time for attempting to defend himself against the five white men who nearly beat him to death in a hate crime.

## Dr. G.B. Burt (Grover Burt)
HILLSBOROUGH, NC 2009

He survived all of this without the slightest bitterness in his heart by adhering to the practice of nonviolence he studied under Coretta Scott King.

When we met Dr. Burt in 2008, he immediately embraced the Music Maker mission with gusto and jumped on a plane, his first flight ever, to Australia to perform in Byron Bay. He told us, "Music Maker has given these musicians the opportunity to share our vision and love for the blues with other people, and this here is worldwide. This is a dream I had when I was young. I intend to do another song called, "Pinch Me and Wake Up," because I can't believe it! Australia and Paris, France! The Music Maker, I love you. Its incredible. I thought all of this was just gone at my age of 77 years. But here I am!"

Dr. Burt loved being with people and never stopped spreading joy, he even called us from his deathbed in Detroit, hoping we could find him a gig nearby. It was impossible not to be affected by this man of love and peace.

## Boo Hanks

Boo Hanks' great-great-grandfather was purchased as a house boy along with a mule in Charleston, SC. They were given as a wedding gift to Colonel Hargrove of Granville County, NC. Boo learned the blues from his father and his large stack of Blind Boy Fuller records. His elders always told him that they were descendants of Abraham Lincoln's mother, Mary Hanks. Boo's family never left the Hargrove Plantation; here he is at his family home where he grew up and later raised his family. His ancestral slave cabin stands nearby. Boo's cousins continue to work the crops for the Hargrove family. Boo worked as a tobacco farmer and at the age of 85 was still working in the fields at harvest.

## Robert Lee Coleman

Columbia, MO 2012

Robert Lee Coleman of Macon, GA, played guitar for Percy Sledge from 1964-1969 and in 1970 he joined James Brown with "The JBs." His bluesy guitar is featured on Brown's albums, *Hot Pants* and *Live at the Apollo*. Like many sidemen, he would travel the world, appear on TV, play the most prestigious venues and come home without a dime. Of course no one back home understood or believed that he was broke. Guys like Robert provided the backbone for all the great R&B artists.

## Cary Morin

HILLSBOROUGH, NC 2013

Cary Morin is a Crow Tribal member from Montana. He is a brilliant guitarist, heartfelt songwriter and soulful singer.

Once he was on tour in Japan and saw an Edward Curtis photograph and was stunned to notice that it was a friend of his great uncle's. He and his father went to the Library of Congress and scoured the Curtis Collection in hopes of finding photos of family members. When he looked at this tintype photograph, it startled him. "My skin looks so brown! I always thought I was paler than my ancestors because they spent more time in the sun! But I look just like them in this photo! I never knew this old photographic process had influenced what the world thought Native Americans looked like."

*"You see my great, great grandfather was a stud. The slave owner viewed him as a bull to breed with his slave women. Every time he got a woman pregnant, his master used to give him a jar of molasses. He would hide that jar from everyone and keep it safe. Eventually, he saved up enough jars to buy himself a cart and a mule. His master used to let him visit other plantations to do business on condition that he would split the jars of molasses. On Sundays, when folks were out and about, he would go to town. When another plantation owner would walk by, he would start to yelling at his mule, lean back and hit him in the jaw. The mule would fall down on his knees. This show of strength helped him get his next job. You see, he trained that donkey to do that! That's how we used to have to get along."*

### Ironing Board Sam (Sammie Moore)

HILLSBOROUGH, NC 2012

In 1965, Sam performed for a year at the Club Del Morocco in Nashville, TN while Jimi Hendrix was playing in the lounge downstairs. He became a true pioneer for performing weekly in the first African American R&B television show, *Night Train*.

In New Orleans he was legendary for his famous stunts, including floating above Jackson Square in a hot air balloon, performing underwater in his homemade giant aquarium, and riding around in a Cadillac that he fitted with crystal chandeliers. He earned his moniker in the early 1960s by inventing the first portable, electronic keyboard, that he called the "button board." It was made from upholstery tacks wired to 64 radio tubes and was mounted on a 2x4 that sat on an ironing board.

## Leyla McCalla

Hillsborough, NC 2011

Leyla McCalla explores the artistry of Langston Hughes. She develops the inherent musicality of his verse further, setting his words to her own melodies. Her sound harks back to the early Creole styles, her voice accompanied by her inventive cello strumming and tenor banjo.

She is also a devoted student of Haitian folk music and performs songs she has collected while visiting her extended family in Haiti.

## Pat Wilder

Hillsborough, NC 2013

The energy heats up as soon as Pat hits the stage. Her deep rocking blues guitar, dancing and original songs bring the audience joy. In 2011, soon after we started working together, she had an aneurysm that burst and caused her to flatline. She spent 60 days in ICU and convalesced for a year. Thank God she recovered and is back out gigging in San Francisco and with the Music Maker Blues Revue.

## Lakota John,
### Layla, Papa John & Tonya Locklear
LUMBERTON, NC 2013

John Lakota Locklear, born in 1997, grew up listening to his dad's music collection. At seven years old, he picked up the harmonica and at nine, his first guitar. Intrigued by the sound of the slide guitar, by ten he had bought himself a glass slide, placed it on his pinky finger and has been sliding ever since. He performs with his Mama Tonya, Papa John and Sister Layla; a proud Lumbee and Oglala Nation family of talented musicians.

The Lumbee Nation includes 50,000 members who call the enchanting area of swamps and cypress trees around Robeson County, NC home. The Oglala Sioux Nation of Pine Ridge, known for its rich historical sites and events, is the eighth largest reservation in the United States. Lakota John & Kin continue to stir our musical Southern stew with their ancestors' ancient harmonies and traditional blues melded together.

## Major Handy

Major Handy was born into a family that has been playing Zydeco as far back as anyone can remember. He had steady work on a luxury cruise ship out of New Orleans until Hurricane Katrina hit. He has worked hard to rebuild his livelihood and can be heard at least three days a week performing around his hometown of Lafayette, LA. He is pictured here with an accordion we helped him purchase for his first show with the Music Maker Revue in Australia.

**Guitar Gabriel**

*"Blues will never die because it is a spirit.*
*It is an up lift and the way you feel it,*
*that is the way it is.*
*And it brings a lot of joy to people.*
*Music is made to make happiness,*
*make you smile and forget your troubles.*
*In the Good Book it says to make a joyful noise.*
*It does not say what kind of noise,*
*just as long as you make one.*
*So that is about the size of it,*
*that is what we are trying to do."*

# About MUSIC MAKER Relief Foundation

Music Maker Relief Foundation is a tax exempt, public charity under IRS code 501(c) 3. Our programs are based in Hillsborough, NC. Our staff of six is supported by a small army of interns and volunteers and governed by a Board of Directors.

Since our founding in 1994 we have assisted and partnered with more than 300 musicians, released more than 150 CDs, and reached over one million people with live performances across the US and in 17 countries around the globe.

The artists we work with are rooted in the Southern musical traditions including blues, gospel, string band and Native American. We target our programs to serve the most vulnerable musicians, those age 55 and older with incomes under $18,000 a year. The sad reality is that many of these musicians are getting by on annual incomes of less than $10,000.

Music Maker takes a holistic approach to fostering creativity and has designed four programs to address the complex challenge of making certain that American roots music will continue to thrive.

Our **Musician Sustenance** program makes grants to help with monthly bills for essential needs including medicine, food and housing, and provides emergency funding in times of crisis.

Our **Musical Development** program helps artists hone their skills and gets them performing to earn income. The first step is to grant a quality musical instrument and work with our professionals to develop their repertoire and stage show, then we book as many gigs as the artist would like to play and help them tour.

Our **Cultural Access** program educates and entertains audiences worldwide with roots and blues music while documenting the artists' work for future generations. Music Maker's educational programming brings artists into public schools and onto college campuses to engage youth to explore their cultural heritage and inspire the love of American music.

The **Next Generation** program builds partnerships between young and veteran roots musicians, fostering the continuation of Southern traditional music among new generations. Through internships, this program also trains the next generation of archivists, documentarians and music industry managers.

# How You Can Help

**Please take part in our mission and keep America's musical traditions thriving!**

Join our mission with a donation or membership in our Listener's Circle and join the worldwide network of artists and listeners united in our quest to keep roots music alive.

Listen to the many free tracks at **musicmaker.org**, and follow us on **Facebook** so you can learn more about the artists we serve, their current work and live performances.
Buy artists' recordings at **shop.musicmaker.org** or on **iTunes**. Your interest inspires our musicians to keep creating.

Share **Music Maker** with your friends and family by bringing them to a show, making a donation in their honor or sending them a gift of music!

Celebrate and experience these living legends at the many festival and club shows they perform across the US and around the world every year.

With your support, **Music Maker** can continue forging partnerships with the pioneering musicians that keep American roots music alive.

**Learn more and purchase
the accompanying CD at
musicmaker.org!**

## About the photography

My father, Allen Hooper Duffy, inspired and nurtured my loves of photography and roots music. He taught me how to develop film and print pictures on a wet table he built in our basement. He gave me a Minolta SRT-101 camera and we took a photography class together. He passed away in 1986 but remains my inspiration.

The photographs in this book are sequenced close to the order in which I met each artist. I apologize to the many musical friends who do not appear in this book due to our printing constraints. They have been equally inspiring and contributed tremendously to our mission. Readers please visit musicmaker.org to learn about all of our artists!

Cameras used were: Nikon 28ti & 35ti, Minolta Maxxum & 50mm, Leica M3, M6 & 35mm, 50mm, Hasselblad & Planar 80mm, Super D Graflex & Graflex 198mm, Wollensack Verito 9 inch Diffused Focus, Home Portrait Graflex & Wollensack Vesta Portrait 11 ½ inch, Sony DSC-F707, Canon 20d & 5d mark II & Canon EF 17-40mm, EF 50mm, 4x5 Wista & Schneider Symmar-S 180mm, 4X5 Graflex View & Rodenstock Imagon 250mm, Deardorff 8x10 & Kodak Ektar 240mm, Lennon Limited, Express RR Lens Whole Plate, Express.

Kodak Tri-X film developed in Kodak D-76 and Rodinal. Tin Type images were created by following John Coffers "The Doers Guide to Wet-Plate Photography." Coffer, J. (2000).

**- Timothy Duffy**